Journey to the Center

Journey to the Center

A Lenten Passage

Thomas Keating

A Crossroad Book
The Crossroad Publishing Company
New York

The Crossroad Publishing Company
370 Lexington Avenue, New York, NY 10017

Acknowledgments will be found on pp. 117-118,
which constitute an extension of the copyright page.

Library of Congress Cataloging-in-Publication Data

Keating, Thomas.
    Journey to the center : a Lenten passage / Thomas Keating.
       p. cm.
    ISBN 0-8245-1703-2
    1. Lent--Prayer-books and devotions--English. I. Title
  BV85.K385 1998   98-22535
  242' . 34--dc21   CIP

1 2 3 4 5 6 7 8 9 10 04 03 02 01 00 99

CONTENTS

THE LENTEN JOURNEY

Lent is the season in which the church as a whole enters into an extended retreat. Jesus went into the desert for forty days and forty nights. The practice of Lent is a participation in Jesus' solitude, silence, and privation.

The forty days of Lent bring into focus a long biblical tradition beginning with the Flood in the Book of Genesis, when rain fell upon the earth for forty days and forty nights. We read about Elijah walking forty days and forty nights to the mountain of God, Mt. Horeb. We read about the forty years that the Israelites wandered through the desert in order to reach the Promised Land. The biblical desert is primarily a place of purification, a place of passage. The biblical desert is not so much a geographical location—a place of sand, stones or sagebrush—as a process of interior purification leading to the complete liberation from the false-self system with its programs for happiness that cannot possibly work.

Jesus deliberately took upon himself the human condition—fragile, broken, alienated from God and other people. A whole program of self-centered concerns has been built up around our instinctual needs and have become energy centers—sources of motivation around which our emotions, thoughts, and behavior patterns circulate like planets around the sun. Whether consciously or unconsciously, these programs for happiness influence our view of the world and our relationship with God, nature, other people, and ourselves. This is the situation that Jesus went into the desert to heal. During Lent our work is to confront these programs for happiness and to detach ourselves from them. The scripture readings chosen for Lent and the example of Jesus encourage us in this struggle for inner freedom and conversion.

—Thomas Keating

REPENTANCE

Joel 2:12-13

Yet even now, says the Lord,
   return to me with all your heart,
with fasting, with weeping, and with mourning;
   rend your hearts and not your clothing.
Return to the Lord, your God,
   for he is gracious and merciful,
slow to anger, and abounding in steadfast love,
   and relents from punishing.

To repent is not to take on afflictive penances like fasting, vigils, flagellation, or whatever else appeals to our generosity. It means *to change the direction in which you are looking for happiness*. That challenge goes to the root of the problem. It is not just a bandage for one or another of the emotional problems.

If we say yes to the invitation to repent, we may experience enormous freedom for a few months or for even a year or two. Our former way of life, in some degree, is cleaned up and certain relationships healed. Then, after a year or two, the dust stirred up by our first conversion settles and the old temptations recur. As the springtime of the spiritual journey turns to summer—and fall and winter—the original enthusiasms begin to wane. At some

11

point, we have to face the fundamental problem, which is the unconscious motivation that is still in place, even after we have chosen the values of the gospel.

The false self is the syndrome of our emotional programs for happiness grown into sources of motivation and made much more complex by the socialization process, and reinforced by our over-identification with our cultural conditioning. Our ordinary thoughts, reactions, and feelings manifest the false self on every level of our conduct. When the false self learns that we have been converted and will now start practicing all the virtues, it has the biggest laugh of a lifetime and dares us, saying, "Just try it!"

Now we experience the full force of the spiritual combat, the struggle with what we want to do and feel we should do, and our incredible inability to carry it out. . . . Such insight is the beginning of the real spiritual journey.

—*Invitation to Love*

Prayer

Come, Holy Spirit, open our hearts to the power of Your Love and set our feet upon the narrow way that leads to eternal Life.

DYING TO THE FALSE SELF

Luke 9:23-25

If any want to become my followers, let them deny themselves and take up their cross daily and follow me. For those who want to save their life will lose it, and those who lose their life for my sake will save it. What does it profit them if they gain the whole world, but lose or forfeit themselves?

Jesus said, "If anyone would come after me, let him deny himself and take up his cross and follow me" (Matthew 16:24). What is this "self"? It is our thoughts, feelings, self-image, and world view. Jesus added, "Whoever would save his life will lose it, and whoever loses his life for my sake, will find it" (Matthew 16:25). That is, he will find eternal life, the Christ-life, welling up within.

Faith is not just the acceptance of abstract propositions about God; it is the total surrender of ourselves to God. In baptism, our false self is put to death and the victory won by Christ is placed at our disposal. The dynamic set off in baptism is meant to increase continuously during the course of our chronological lives and lead to the experience of the risen life of Christ within us. In the Christian view, death is thus an integral part of living. Dying to the false self is the movement from a lower form of life to a higher one; from a lower state of consciousness to a higher state of consciousness; from a weak faith to a faith that is strong, penetrating, and unifying.

Participation in the life of Christ means coming to know and love the person of Jesus. The humanity of Christ is our starting point and the door into his divinity. Jesus said, "I am the door of the sheepfold. If anyone enters by me, he shall go in and out and find pasture" (John 10:7-9). We enter through the knowledge and love of Christ's humanity into the sheepfold of his divinity, where he invites us to rest in oneness of spirit. The new person that comes to birth in that deep interior rest manifests Christ in the place and time in which he or she lives.

—The Heart of the World

Prayer

Holy Spirit of God, through Your Gift of Knowledge, may all of our self-centered programs for happiness be laid to rest in the sure conviction that true happiness can be found in You alone.

THE NEW WINE

Matthew 9:14-17

*The disciples of John came to [Jesus], saying,
"Why do we and the Pharisees fast often, but
your disciples do not fast?" And Jesus said to
them, "The wedding guests cannot mourn as
long as the bridegroom is with them, can they?
The days will come when the bridegroom is
taken away from them, and then they will fast.
No one sews a piece of unshrunk cloth on an
old cloak, for the patch pulls away from the
cloak, and a worse tear is made. Neither is new
wine put into old wineskins; otherwise, the
skins burst, and the wine is spilled, and the
skins are destroyed; but new wine is put into
fresh wineskins, and so both are preserved."*

New wine is a marvelous image of the Holy Spirit. As
we move to the intuitive level of consciousness through
contemplative prayer, the energy of the Spirit cannot be
contained in the old structures. They are not flexible
enough. They may have to be left aside or adapted. The
new wine as a symbol of the Spirit has a tendency to stir
people up; for that reason, the Fathers of the Church called

it "sober intoxication." Although its exuberance is subdued, it breaks out of categories and cannot be contained in neat boxes.

Jesus points out to John's disciples that they have a good practice but are too attached to fasting as a structure. The wine of the Spirit that Jesus brings will not fit into their narrow ideas. They must expand their views. Otherwise, the new wine of the Gospel will give them trouble. It will burst the narrow confines of their mindsets, and both what they have and what they are trying to receive will be lost.

Jesus suggests a solution: "Put the new wine into new wineskins." The new wine of the Gospel is manifested by the fruits of the Spirit which are nine aspects of the mind of Christ. If the new wine is to be preserved, new structures have to be found that are more appropriate than the old ones.

—*Awakenings*

Prayer

Come, Holy Spirit; create in us the nine-fold aspects of the mind of Christ that St. Paul calls the Fruits of the Spirit, especially the peace which surpasses all understanding.

I CALL SINNERS

Luke 5:30-32

The Pharisees and their scribes were complaining to [Jesus'] disciples, saying, "Why do you eat and drink with tax collectors and sinners?" Jesus answered, "Those who are well have no need of a physician, but those who are sick; I have come to call not the righteous but sinners to repentance."

When Jesus said, "I've come to call not the self-righteous, but sinners," this was big news. This statement warns those who pursue the spiritual journey to be aware of the serious disease that afflicts them. Contemplative prayer is a kind of antibiotic for this disease. Notice the heavy irony in Jesus' words. "I have come to call not the self-righteous, but sinners." Everybody suffers from the disease of the human condition (original sin) and is therefore a sinner. It is just a matter of degree. People who think they are not sick, who regard themselves as righteous or God's greatest gifts to humanity, are the subject of Jesus' ironic statement: "People in good health do not need a doctor. Sick people do." To paraphrase: "If you are willing to recognize the disease of the false self, I am at your service."

17

This juxtaposition of people who know they are sinners
and those who do not know they are sinners though they
are just as sick occurs in the parables. Take the prodigal
son. As soon as the profligate comes home, he is treated to
a celebration. . . .

The sacrament of reconciliation is not only the confes-
sion of sins, but the celebration that our sins have been
forgiven. It is the same kind of event that the prodigal son
celebrated. . . . Self-righteous people cannot understand
how God can celebrate the return of profligates, crooks and
extortionists just because they seem to have turned over a
new leaf. The respectability that tends to cling to us when
we lead a fairly good life hides our own tendency to prefer
ourselves to the rights and needs of others.

Obvious sinners seem to be in a better situation. When
they hit bottom, where else can they go except into the
mercy of God? We could go there without having to hit
bottom if we recognized that we too are sinners in need of
healing.

—Awakenings

Prayer

*O Holy Spirit, free us from our idealized image
of ourselves which overreacts to daily life with
feelings of self-exaltation or self-depreciation.
Guide us to a true and humble knowledge and
acceptance of who we really are.*

TEMPTATION

Luke 4:1-2

Jesus, full of the Holy Spirit, returned from the Jordan and was led by the Spirit in the wilderness, where for forty days he was tempted by the devil.

Jesus appears in the desert as the representative of the human race. He bears within himself the experience of the human predicament in its raw intensity. Hence, he is vulnerable to the temptations of Satan. Satan in the New Testament means the Enemy or the Adversary, a mysterious and malicious spirit that seems to be more than a mere personification of our unconscious evil tendencies. The temptations of Satan are allowed by God to help us confront our own evil tendencies. If relatives and friends fail to bring out the worst in us, Satan is always around to finish the job. Self-knowledge is experiential; it tastes the full depths of human weakness.

In the desert Jesus is tempted by the primitive instincts of human nature. Satan first addresses Jesus' security/survival needs, which constitute the first energy level: "If you are the Son of God, command these stones to become bread."

After fasting forty days and forty nights, Jesus must have been desperately hungry. His reply to Satan's suggestion is that it is not up to him to protect or to save himself; it is up to the Father to provide for him. "Not on bread alone does one live, but on every word that comes from the mouth of God." God has promised to provide for everyone who trusts in him. Jesus refuses to take his own salvation in hand and waits for God to rescue him.

The devil then took Jesus to the holy city, set him on the parapet of the temple and suggested, "If you are the Son of God, throw yourself down. Scripture has it, 'He will bid his angels take care of you; with their hands they will support you, that you may not stumble upon a stone!'"

In other words, "If you are the Son of God, manifest your power as a wonderworker. Jump off this skyscraper. When you stand up and walk, everybody will regard you as a bigshot and bow down before you." This is the temptation to love fame and public esteem.

Affection/esteem constitute the center of gravity of the second energy center. Everybody needs a measure of acceptance and affirmation. In the path from infancy to adulthood, if these needs are denied, one seeks compensation for the real or imagined deprivations of early childhood. The greater the deprivation, the greater the neurotic drive for compensation.

In the text, Satan subtly quotes Psalm 90, the great theme song of Lent, a psalm of boundless confidence in God under all circumstances. He suggests that if Jesus leaps off the temple parapet, God will have to protect him. Jesus responds, "You shall not put the Lord your God to the test." In other words, no matter how many proofs of God's special love we may have, we may not take our salvation into our own hands. Jesus rejects the happiness program that seeks the glorification of the self as a wonderworker or spiritual luminary.

The third energy center is the desire to control events and to have power over others. Satan took Jesus to a lofty mountain and displayed before him all the kingdoms of the world, promising, "All these I will bestow on you if you prostrate yourself in homage before me." The temptation to worship Satan in exchange for the symbols of unlimited power is the last-ditch effort of the false self to achieve its own invulnerability and immortality. Jesus replied, "Away with you, Satan. Scripture says, 'You shall do homage to the Lord your God; him alone shall you adore.'" Adoration of God is the antidote to pride and lust for power. Service of others and not domination is the path to true happiness.

Thus, out of love for us, Jesus experienced the temptations of the first three energy centers. Each Lent he invites us to join him in the desert and to share his trials.

—*The Mystery of Christ*

Prayer

Holy Spirit of Truth, teach us how to relinquish our over-identification with our bodies, feelings, emotional programs for happiness, intellectual powers, cultural conditioning, and idealized image of ourselves. Thus, may we be free just to be our true selves and to do Your will.

CONSENT TO GOD

Matthew 25:34-36

Come, you that are blessed by my Father,
inherit the kingdom prepared for you from the
foundation of the world; for I was hungry and
you gave me food, I was thirsty and you gave
me something to drink, I was a stranger and
you welcomed me, I was naked and you gave
me clothing, I was sick and you took care of
me, I was in prison and you visited me.

The spiritual journey is a training in consent to God's presence and to all reality. Basically this is what true humility is. The divine action invites us to make the consents that we were unable to make in childhood and growing up because of the circumstances that surrounded our early lives.

This brings us to a paradigm for the spiritual journey that sheds a great deal of light on the positive aspects of grace, which not only heals the emotional damage of a lifetime, but also empowers us to enter on the path of unconditional love, even from the beginning of our conversion. Jesus emphasized this approach to divine union when he said, "Love one another as I have loved you."

The theologian John S. Dunne has suggested that the

stages of the spiritual journey correspond to the passage of human life from birth to death. At each major stage of that development, God asks us to make an appropriate consent.

In childhood, God asks us to consent to the basic goodness of our nature with all its parts. As children we experience our own faculties, develop imagination, memory, and language, and learn to relate to family and peers. In these years we are asked to accept the basic goodness of our being as a gift from God and to be grateful for it.

In early adolescence, God asks us to accept the full development of our being by activating our talents and creative energies. Puberty actualizes the physical side of a much broader energy: our capacity to relate to other people, to emerge out of the isolated world of a child, and to begin to assume responsibility for ourselves and for our relationships.

In early adulthood, God invites us to make a third consent: to accept the fact of our nonbeing and the diminutions of self that occur through illness, old age, and death.

The fourth consent is the consent to be transformed. We might think that everybody would be eager to make this one, but even the holiest people are inclined to say, "Let's not rush into this." The transforming union requires consent to the death of the false self, and the false self is the only self we know. Whatever its inconveniences, it is at least familiar. Some of us are more afraid of the death of the false self than of physical death.

This gradual training in consent is the school of divine love in which God invites us to accept the divine plan to share the divine life with us in a way that transcends all that the human imagination can foresee. We do not make these consents as ends in themselves, but rather to the will of God present in these things. We consent to God and to his will both in the enjoyment and in the surrender of his gifts.

—*Invitation to Love*

Prayer

O Holy Spirit, through Your unfailing
inspiration, may we consent ever more fully to
Your Presence and action within us.

PRAYER

Matthew 6:7-13

*When you are praying, do not heap up empty
phrases as the Gentiles do; for they think that
they will be heard because of their many words.
Do not be like them, for your Father knows
what you need before you ask him.*
    Pray, then in this way:
    Our Father in heaven,
        hallowed be your name.
    Your kingdom come.
    Your will be done,
        on earth as it is in heaven.
    Give us this day our daily bread.
    And forgive us our debts,
        as we also have forgiven our debtors.
    And do not bring us to the time of trial,
        but rescue us from the evil one.

Prayer is a large umbrella. There are many kinds of
prayer and many ways of expressing it. Fundamentally, it is
a response to God's invitation to turn our minds and hearts
to him. The classical formulas are that of Evagrius, which
is the laying aside of thoughts; and that of St. John Dama-
scene, which is conversation of the mind with God. By

"mind" St. John means the spiritual faculties of intellect and will. Sometimes this interior movement needs to be expressed in words or concepts, but to be true prayer, it does not have to be expressed by words or concepts.

The Fathers of the Church and the great spiritual masters of the Christian tradition have elaborated on various levels and degrees of prayer. We may also think of prayer as a conversation with God, which deepens as one becomes more and more devoted to him. That deepening does not prevent us from expressing prayer spontaneously on every level of our being, from the spoken word of prayer to the simple movement of the will, which the *Cloud of Unknowing* calls a "gentle stirring of love." This simple movement of the will is scarcely perceptible to our attention, but at the deepest level of our being, it unites us more intimately to the Holy Spirit than any other form of prayer. For, as St. John of the Cross teaches, the Spirit is the sole mover at that deep level of interior silence and works powerfully without our being aware of what is happening.

—*The Heart of the World*

Prayer

O Holy Spirit, may Your Light open our minds to the truth and strengthen our wills to accept the truth without wavering.

CONVERSION

Jonah 3:6

When the news reached the king of Nineveh, he rose from his throne, removed his robe, covered himself with sackcloth, and sat in ashes.

The process of conversion begins with genuine openness to change—to be open to the possibility that just as natural life evolves, so our spiritual life is evolving. Our psychological world is the result of natural growth, events over which we had no control in early childhood and grade school. Grace, which is the presence and action of Christ in our lives, invites us to be ready to let go of where we are now and to be open to the new values that are born when we penetrate to a new understanding of the Gospel and how it applies concretely to our daily lives. Moreover, Jesus calls us to repent not just once; it is a message that keeps recurring.

It is a gilt-edged invitation. Each time you consent to an enhancement of faith, your world changes and all your relationships have to be adjusted to the new perspective and the new light that has been given you. Our relationship to ourselves, to Jesus Christ, to our neighbor, to the Church—to God—all change. It is the end of the world we have previously known and lived in. Sometimes the Spirit of God deliberately shatters one of these worlds. If we have depended upon them to go to God, it may feel as if we have lost God. We may have doubts about God's very existence. Such doubts may be the best thing that ever happened to us. It is not the true God of faith we have doubts about, but only the God of our limited concepts or dependencies; this god never existed anyway.

And so the second part of Jesus' message is very important. If you repent and are willing to change, or are willing to let God change you, the kingdom of God is close; in fact, you have it; it is within you and you can begin to enjoy it. The kingdom of God belongs to those who are poor in spirit, who have let go of their possessive attitude toward everything, including God.

—*Contemplative Outreach News*, Winter, 1988

Prayer

Holy Spirit of God, give us the grace of true sorrow for our sins and the sure hope of pardon for all of our sins.

FEAR OF GOD

Esther 14:1, 3-5

Then Queen Esther, seized with deadly anxiety, fled to the Lord. She prayed to the Lord God of Israel, and said: "O my Lord, you only are our king; help me, who am alone and have no helper but you, for my danger is in my hand. Ever since I was born I have heard in the tribe of my family that you, O Lord, took Israel out of all the nations, and our ancestors from among all their forebears, for an everlasting inheritance, and that you did for them all that you promised."

The biblical term "fear of God" does not refer to the emotion of fear. Fear of God is a technical term in the Bible meaning the right relationship with God. The right relationship with God is to trust him. The right relationship with God involves reverence and awe for God's transcendence and immanence as well as trust in his goodness and compassion. To envisage what the biblical fear of God actually means, imagine a child at Christmastime in a huge department store. The top floor, the size of a whole city block, is filled with toys. When the child emerges from the elevator into the wonderland of desirable objects, her eyes

grow bigger and bigger. She looks to the left and to the
right, seeing everything her heart has ever desired: skis,
teddy bears, doll houses, toys, sleds, electric trains, com-
puters. She wants to go in every direction at once. She is so
enthralled that she does not know where to start. She wants
to grasp everything and take it home. The biblical fear of
God is similar. We feel ourselves invited into a mystery
that contains everything our hearts could possibly desire.
We experience the fascination of the Ultimate Mystery
rather than fear of the unknown. We want to grasp or be
grasped by the mystery of God's presence that opens
endlessly in every direction.

—Invitation to Love

Prayer

Come, Holy Spirit, be present in time of
temptation and gently coax our timid hearts to
trust in You.

PURIFICATION

Ezekiel 18:21-22

*But if the wicked turn away from all their sins
that they have committed and keep all my
statutes and do what is lawful and right, they
shall surely live; they shall not die. None of the
transgressions that they have committed shall
be remembered against them; for the righteous-
ness that they have done they shall live.*

In religious circles there is a cliché that describes the
divine purification as "a battering from without and a
boring from within." God goes after our accumulated junk
with something equivalent to a compressor and starts
digging through our defense mechanisms, revealing the
secret corners that hide the unacceptable parts of ourselves.
We may think it is the end of our relationship with God.
Actually, it is an invitation to a new depth of relationship
with God. A lot of emptying and healing has to take place
if we are to be responsive to the sublime communications
of God. The full transmission of divine life cannot come
through and be fully heard if the static of the false self is
too loud.

Once we start the spiritual journey, God is totally on
our side. Everything works together for our good. If we can

31

believe this, we can save ourselves an enormous amount of trouble. Purification of the unconscious is an important part of the journey. The decision to choose the values of the gospel does not touch the unconscious motivation that is firmly in place by age three or four, and more deeply entrenched by the age of reason. As long as the false self with its emotional programs for happiness is in place, we tend to appropriate any progress in the journey to ourselves.

The experience of God's love and the experience of our weaknesses are correlative. These are the two poles that God works with as he gradually frees us from immature ways of relating to him. The experience of our desperate need for God's healing is the measure in which we experience his infinite mercy. The deeper the experience of God's mercy, the more compassion we will have for others.

—Invitation to Love

Prayer

*Holy Spirit of God, may the refining fire of
Your Love reach into the hidden places of our
inmost being and make us one spirit with You.*

ONENESS OF CREATION

Matthew 5:43-45

*You have heard that it was said, "You shall love
your neighbor and hate your enemy." But I say
to you, Love your enemies and pray for those
who persecute you, so that you may be children
of your Father in heaven; for he makes his sun
rise on the evil and on the good, and sends rain
on the righteous and on the unrighteous.*

One of the things that Centering Prayer, as it deepens,
will affect is our intuition of the oneness of the human
family, and indeed, the oneness of all creation. As one
moves into one's own inmost being, one comes into contact
with what is the inmost being of everyone else. Although
each of us retains his or her own unique personhood, we
are necessarily associated with the Divine–human person
who has taken the whole human family to himself in such a
way as to be the inmost reality of each individual member
of it. And so, when one is praying in one's inmost being, in
one's spirit, one is praying, so to speak, in everyone else's
spirit.

In the Eucharist, we are not only joined to Jesus Christ
present with his whole being under the symbols of bread
and wine, but we believe we are joined with all other

Christians, with every member of the human race, and indeed with the whole of creation. Jesus Christ in his divinity is in the hearts of all men and women and in the heart of all creation, sustaining everything in being. This mystery of oneness enables us to emerge from the Eucharist with a refined inward eye, and invites us to perceive the mystery of Christ everywhere and in every thing. He who is hidden from our senses and intellect in his divine nature becomes more and more transparent to the eyes of faith—to the consciousness that is being transformed. Christ's Spirit in us perceives the same Spirit in others.

The Eucharist is the celebration of life, the dance of the divine in human form. We are part of that dance. Each of us is a continuation of Christ's incarnation insofar as we are living Christ's life in our own lives—or rather, instead of our own lives. The Eucharist is the summary of all creation coming together in a single hymn of praise and thanksgiving. In the Eucharist all creation is transformed into the body of Christ, united with his divine Person, and thrust into the depths of the Father for ever and ever. Even material creation has become divine in him.

—*Contemplative Outreach News*, Winter, 1997

Prayer

O Holy Spirit, through our growing union with Jesus, help us to practice the utmost charity toward the members of our family, toward our respective communities, and toward the whole human family.

THE TRANSFIGURATION

Matthew 17:1-5

*Jesus took with him Peter and James and his
brother John and led them up a high mountain,
by themselves. And he was transfigured before
them, and his face shone like the sun, and his
clothes became dazzling white. Suddenly there
appeared to them Moses and Elijah, talking
with him. Then Peter said to Jesus, "Lord, it is
good for us to be here; if you wish, I will make
three dwellings here, one for you, one for
Moses, and one for Elijah." While he was still
speaking, suddenly a bright cloud overshad-
owed them, and from the cloud a voice said,
"This is my Son, the Beloved; with him I am
well pleased; listen to him!"*

Jesus' going up the mountain to be transfigured points
to the transformation that we receive on the spiritual
journey after a time of purification. After enduring the
inner desert of purification, God refreshes us with transforming experiences. The mountain of the Transfiguration
is not just a place of retreat. It symbolizes the experience of
spiritual awakening that is the purpose of the practice of
contemplative prayer.

The first clear indication that contemplative prayer is
becoming established in oneself is the attraction to solitude. This attraction comes from the refining of our faculties through the dismantling of our emotional programs for
happiness and the consequent reduction of the static that
they cause as everyday life keeps frustrating them. In this
event the emotional programs of the three apostles have
been left on the plain, so to speak, at least temporarily.
Their attraction to solitude is symbolized by Jesus leading
them up the mountain. It is the first sign of their spiritual
awakening.

We begin to access the mystery of God's presence
through a similar attraction, even though the particular
mountain we are on—a retreat or our daily period of
prayer—may not bring us any satisfaction whatsoever. Like
an irresistible magnet, the attraction for solitude draws us
without our knowing where it is coming from. We wait
patiently upon God day after day in prayer and stumble
along in our ordinary occupations.

On this holy mountain, Jesus exploded into a presence
that overwhelmed the disciples. . . . Jesus turned into light;
even his clothes became saturated with it. A kind of glory
suffused itself into their senses both inward and outward. If
we perceive the divine presence in some facsimile to this
clarity, we are fascinated, absorbed, and delighted. Peter's
response was to want to stay there forever. The more
profound the experience of union, the more one cannot
help but wish to prolong it.

Just as the disciples are beginning to experience the delight of the divine presence in the person of Jesus, a cloud suddenly overshadows them. The cloud is the symbol of the unknowing that we enter as a habitual state through the regular practice of contemplative prayer. Suddenly a voice from the cloud resounded, saying, "This is my beloved Son, listen to him." Listen not just to his words to which they had been listening when they were on the plain, but "listen to *him*," the divine person who is speaking to you. Listen to the divine presence that is incarnate in this human being. Listen to the infinite Silence out of which the incarnate Word emerges and to which it returns.

The grace of the Transfiguration is not just a vision of glory, an isolated experience of divine consolation, however exalted. Of course, such an experience has immense value. But its primary purpose is something greater: to empower us to live in the presence of God and to see the radiance of that presence in all events, people, the cosmos, and in ourselves.

—*Reawakenings*

Prayer

O Holy Spirit, free us from all the emotional programs for happiness that feed our false selves and grant us the restfulness of detachment from their restless energy.

ORIGINAL SIN

Daniel 9:4-6

*Ah, Lord, great and awesome God, keeping
covenant and steadfast love with those who
love you and keep your commandments, we
have sinned and done wrong, acted wickedly
and rebelled, turning aside from your
commandments and ordinances. We have not
listened to your servants the prophets, who
spoke in your name to our kings, our princes,
and our ancestors, and to all the people of
the land.*

The term "original sin" is a way of describing the
universal experience of coming to full reflective self-
consciousness without the certitude of personal union with
God. This gives rise to our intimate sense of incompletion,
dividedness, isolation, and guilt. The cultural consequences
of these alienations are instilled in us from earliest childhood and passed on from one generation to the next. The
urgent need to escape from the profound insecurity of this
situation, when unchecked, gives rise to insatiable desires
for pleasure, possessions, and power. On the social level, it
gives rise to violence, war, and institutional injustice.

The particular consequences of original sin include all the self-serving habits that have been woven into our personalities from the time we were conceived; all the harm that other people have done to us knowingly or unknowingly at an age when we could not defend ourselves; and the methods we acquired, many of them now unconscious, to ward off the pain of unbearable situations. This constellation of prerational reactions is the foundation of the false self. The false self develops in opposition to the true self. Its center of gravity is the self as separate from God and others, and hence turned in on itself.

—Invitation to Love

Prayer

Creator Spirit, You have bestowed on us our basic human goodness which nothing can destroy. Give us the grace to overcome every obstacle from without and every evil inclination from within, to being fully human and to becoming divinized by Your transforming Love.

DEEP LISTENING

Isaiah 1:10

Hear the word of the Lord,
you rulers of Sodom!
Listen to the teaching of our God,
you people of Gomorrah!

Christ is the full expression of the Father. Jesus, the humanity of Christ, is the full manifestation of all that the Father is, insofar as this can be expressed in human nature. Jesus is the living symbol of God's love, mercy, and incredible tenderness toward his creatures. He is also the way that God communicates divine life to us. The actions that Christ performed during his earthly life expressed his inner dispositions, and none more completely than his passion, death, and resurrection, toward which the whole of his life was oriented. By knowing the historical Jesus, by listening to his Word in the Gospel and in the events of his life, we learn, little by little, to interiorize his teaching and his actions and begin to understand them. This is what we might call *deep listening*.

But like Mary of Bethany at the feet of Jesus, it is not enough just to listen to his words with our ears and to reflect on them with our reason. This is only an essential preliminary to getting acquainted with him, as in getting acquainted with any new friend. If we are really interested in making this friendship grow, we will find out all we can about him, spend time in prayer, and put his teaching into practice. As we reflect on the Word of God and the humanity of Jesus, we begin to listen with the ears of our hearts. Just as we can converse with someone on the level of words, so we can commune with someone on the level of silence. If we are quite closely acquainted, we can do it just by sitting together and communing without words. Anyone who has a close friend knows this experience.

But there is an even deeper level of conversation than communion, and that is *unity*. It is to this level that the Word of God is ultimately addressed. This is the capacity to listen with our whole being. Total response to Christ is only possible when we hear his word on every level of our being, including the deepest level, which is that of interior silence. It is at this level that his Word is most powerful and most creative; action that emerges from that silence is effective.

—The Heart of the World

Prayer

> *O Holy Spirit, under Your sure guidance, help*
> *us to listen to the words of Scripture that You*
> *have inspired and to penetrate their meaning at*
> *ever-deepening levels of understanding,*
> *insight, and response.*

LIBERATE THE TRUE SELF

Psalm 31:4-5

Take me out of the net that is hidden for me,
for you are my refuge.
Into your hand I commit my spirit;
you have redeemed me, O Lord, faithful
God.

Because of the damage resulting from our fallen human condition, we are not normally in touch with our spiritual nature. Our actual psychological consciousness on a day-to-day level consists of our homemade self manifesting itself and not God.

The spiritual journey is initiated when we become aware that our ordinary psychological consciousness is dominated by the false self with its programs for happiness and over-identification with our cultural conditioning. The spiritual journey involves an inner change of attitude beginning with the recognition of being out of contact with our spiritual nature and our true self, and taking means to return. Only then can our true self and the potentiality that God has given us to live the divine life be manifested. Contemplative service is action coming from the true self, from our inmost being.

To liberate our true self is an enormous undertaking and a program that takes time. Centering Prayer is completely at the service of this program. It would be a mistake to think of Centering Prayer as a mere rest period or a period of relaxation, although it sometimes provides these things. Neither is it a journey to bliss. You might get a little bliss along the way, but you will also have to endure the wear and tear of the discipline of cultivating interior silence.

Thinking our usual thoughts is the chief way that human nature has devised to hide from the unconscious. So when our minds begin to quiet down in Centering Prayer, up comes the emotional debris of a lifetime in the form of gradual and sometimes dramatic realizations of what the false self is, and how this homemade self that we constructed in early childhood to deal with unbearable pain became misdirected from genuine human values into seeking substitutes for God. Images that don't really have any existence except in our imagination are projected on other people instead of facing head-on their source in ourselves.

Just think of the beatitudes that Jesus proclaims. The capacity to practice them is within us as part of the patrimony of Baptism. Similarly, the Seven Gifts of the Spirit and the Fruits of the Spirit enumerated by Paul in Galatians 5 are vibrating within us all the time. But they are mediated through the various levels of the psyche; we don't experience their power until they are awakened through the discipline of deep prayer.

When you emerge from Centering Prayer, the present moment is what happens when you open your eyes. You have been in the present moment of prayer when you were completely open to the divine life and action within you. Now you get up out of the chair and you continue daily life. This is where attentiveness to the content of the present moment is a way of putting order into the myriad occupations, thoughts and events of daily life. Attention to this context simply means to do what you are doing. This was one of the principal recommendations of the Desert Fathers and Mothers of the fourth century. The disciple would come for instruction and say, "I am interested in finding the true self and becoming a contemplative. What should I do?" The Desert guides would reply in the most prosaic language. "Do what you're doing." Which means, bring your attention to the present moment and to whatever is its immediate content and keep it there.

—*Contemplative Outreach News*, Spring, 1996

Prayer

Creator Spirit, through Your Gift of Wisdom,
may we come to know our true Self and its
source in Your unconditional Love.

SOLIDARITY WITH THE POOR

Luke 16:19-21

*There was a rich man who was dressed in
purple and fine linen and who feasted
sumptuously every day. And at his gate lay a
poor man named Lazarus, covered with sores,
who longed to satisfy his hunger with what fell
from the rich man's table; even the dogs would
come and lick his sores.*

In this parable, the sudden reversal of roles and expectations so characteristic of Jesus' teaching is once again
manifested. Two extreme situations are juxtaposed. A rich
man dressed in purple, symbol of the upper classes and
power, feasted not just well, but sumptuously—and not just
on feast days, but every day. At the gate to his estate lay
Lazarus the beggar. In the popular mindset of the time
beggars were considered responsible for their miserable
plight. Poverty was looked upon as a punishment for sin
and for that reason, the hearers would be thinking, "It's his
own fault."

The sin of the rich man could not have been his wealth
as such, since Abraham too was a rich man and found favor
with God, as the book of Genesis attests. The rich man's

fate suggests that his sin was his failure to pass through the gate of his estate and to respond to the desperate need of the beggar. The parable attacks the complacency of our divisions between rich and poor, the socially acceptable and the socially outcast. The gate symbolizes the grace that enables us to love our neighbor—everyone—as ourselves. The rich man stayed in his enclosure. His failure to go through the gate and to enter into solidarity with the one in need was the particular cause of his undoing.

Gates can be barriers or passageways into solidarity with others. In whatever way the rich man obtained his goods, whether through junk bonds or other means of getting rich quick, he failed to pass through the gate of his private interests and concerns to identify with someone whose situation was desperate and whom he could easily have helped. In the next life things will be reversed. If the rich man had gone through the gate to reach out to the beggar and had not simply used it as a barrier to protect himself and his property, his fate would have been quite different. God does not set up barriers. We do. Our relationship to our local community and to the human family as a whole determines whether we are in the kingdom or out of it, both now and in the next life.

To be in the kingdom is to participate in God's solidarity with the poor by sharing with them the good things that have been given to us. In the New Testament the great sin is to be deaf to the cry of the poor whether that cry springs from emotional, material, or spiritual need. Although we cannot help but partake in some degree in social injustice because we live in this world, we must constantly reach out in concrete and practical ways to those in need. Divine love is not a feeling, but a choice. It is to show mercy. The rich man, although he saw the beggar starving at his doorstep and could easily have reached out to him, just went on eating, drinking, and reading his *Wall Street Journal.*

—*The Kingdom of God Is Like . . .*

Prayer

Holy Spirit of God, grant us an ever-deepening relationship with the living Christ and the practical caring for others that flows from that union.

JOY IN HARDSHIP

Matthew 21:42

*The stone that the builders rejected
has become the cornerstone;
this was the Lord's doing
and it is amazing in our eyes.*

Paul tells us to look to Christ, "who for the joy set before him endured the cross, despising the shame" (Hebrews 12:2). This is an important insight in trying to understand suffering. What is normally experienced as painful at one level of our evolving consciousness is not necessarily experienced as painful when we move to a higher level on the ladder of consciousness. It is obvious among the saints of all religions that, although they led incredibly difficult and arduous lives, they experienced joy in those very hardships. Hardship itself seems to have become joy. The same kind of life would have meant intolerable suffering for the average person.

Thus, we have to understand first of all what is meant by "suffering," and then relate it to the person who is undergoing it before making a judgment. It is misleading to think that all aches and pains are going to disappear as one climbs the ladder of consciousness. On the other hand, one's attitude toward suffering is going to change. It may

48

change to such a degree that the experience itself becomes
a joy, not for its own sake, but because it is perceived to be
a participation in the mystery of Christ's passion—a way of
sacrificing oneself in order to express, to the utmost
degree, one's dedication to God. As one comes to know
God more intimately, the heart expands, and the desire for
union with him tends to put all obstacles and hardships into
the shade; to make them seem, while nonetheless real, not
worth thinking about.

—The Heart of the World

Prayer

*Creator Spirit, breathe into our wounded
hearts and minds Your healing Gifts of
forgiveness, understanding, and wisdom.*

THE PRODIGAL SON

Luke 15:31-32

*Then the father said [to the elder son], "Son,
you are always with me, and all that is mine is
yours. But we had to celebrate and rejoice,
because this brother of yours was dead and has
come to life; he was lost and has been found."*

This parable is obviously intended to subvert one of the
favorite themes in the Old Testament—namely, that of the
chosen and the rejected. Because of the older son's misconduct toward the father, the hearers are expecting the story
of Jacob and Esau to be repeated. Jacob, the younger son,
was chosen by God while Esau, the elder son, to whom the
inheritance legally belonged, was rejected. The expectation
is that the elder son in this story is also going to be rejected, and the hearers, who would have identified by now
with the younger son, can rejoice along with him in being
God's specially chosen people.

The conduct of the father, however, effectively de-
stroys the idea of Israel as the chosen people. Instead of
rejecting the elder son for his disrespect, the father affirms,
"You are always with me. Everything that I have is yours."
The elder son thus is assured of his share of the inheritance
in spite of his misconduct. Just as the younger son is

received back into the family in spite of dissipating his father's livelihood, so the elder son, who has just broken the fourth commandment by his insolent disrespect, is restored to favor. The father thus disregards the offenses of *both* sons. He puts completely aside his personal honor and the legal code. He shows himself equally disinterested in the immorality of his younger son and in the offensive self-righteousness that is the preoccupation of his elder son.

What emerges as the primary concern of the father in this parable? It is to unite his two sons: to bring them together in love. Both are guilty of serious failings and he wants to forgive them both. This father's chief concern is not justice but mercy. The father communicates unconditional love to his two sons so that they in turn may show mercy to each other. According to Jesus, his heavenly Father is not especially interested in legal codes and in conventional morality. He seeks the unity of the human family, the removal of divisions and barriers, and the triumph of compassion by manifesting the maternal values, symbolized in that culture by nourishment and overflowing affection.

The parable must have left the Jewish audience with their mouths open in astonishment. What they thought was their major claim to God's protection and love, his free election of them as his chosen people, is profoundly undermined by this parable. The fact is that everyone is chosen. This includes both public sinners, who know that they have offended God, and the self-righteous who deny their complicity in sin. This father forgives both but commands them to live together in peace and common concern—the kind of concern that the Father has shown in sending his Son into the world as the sign of his forgiveness of everything and everyone.

—*The Kingdom of God Is Like* . . .

Prayer

Father, You forgave the Prodigal Son for his wild pursuit of pleasure, squandering in the process the inheritance You had given him. You forgave the Elder Son for his self-righteous condemnation of his younger brother and of Your tender forgiveness of him. You insisted only that they live together as Your children in peace. May we know Your infinite mercy and share it with each other, both as individuals and as nations, races, religions, ethnic groups, neighbors, households, and families.

THE BARREN FIG TREE

Luke 13:6-9

*A man had a fig tree planted in his vineyard;
and he came looking for fruit on it and found
none. So he said to the gardener, "See here!
For three years I have come looking for fruit
on this fig tree, and still I find none. Cut it
down! Why should it be wasting the soil?" He
replied, "Sir, let it alone for one more year,
until I dig around it and put manure on it. If it
bears fruit next year, well and good; but if not,
you can cut it down."*

What are we left with at the conclusion of this parable?
A tree that is good for nothing. The gardener offers to
shovel manure around it, but there is no indication that any
new growth will actually occur. This tree and its predicament are striking symbols of daily life, especially when our
efforts to do good fail or seem to be fruitless, our prayer
periods are as dry as dust, and nothing ever happens. In
addition, there is no sense of God's presence in daily life,
no enlightenment experience, while our faults continue,
people blame us unjustly, and disappointments multiply.
Our spiritual life seems to be dead. What are we to do? The
parable seems to say, just keep waiting.

This parable hints that it does not matter if we do not succeed in our own estimation or in that of others. The divine presence is so present that nothing can take it from us. Of course, we can still reject God, but someone who is seeking God is not about to do that. When we realize the fact of God's closeness, success and failure are relativized. We simply do what we can: that is, we throw a little manure—symbol of our fruitless efforts—on the old stick. Of course it is not going to grow, because it is dead. But in some mysterious way, because of God's solidarity with us in everyday life, something much more important happens.

—The Kingdom of God Is Like . . .

Prayer

Holy Spirit of God, without You there is no divine life in us, nor any virtue. Create in us a conscious relationship with You.

THE GRACE OF WEAKNESS

Luke 4:28-29

When they heard this, all in the synagogue
were filled with rage. They got up, drove him
out of the town, and led him to the brow of the
hill on which their town was built, so that they
might hurl him off the cliff.

Ministry, especially a good one, is a losing game. Paul details the long list of his difficulties, including "a thorn in the flesh" that was interfering with his peace of mind. He kept praying to God to free him from the problem. One would think that God would respond favorably to such a great apostle, make things a little easier for him, or even provide him with the red carpet service. Paul was traveling all over the known world of his time spreading the kingdom of God, and what does he get? Shipwreck, imprisonment, stoning, rejection, persecution, and the betrayal of false brethren. Why could not God, infinitely powerful, do something to smooth the way for the divine message?

Difficulties are a stumbling block for everyone, especially when one is working for God. We cannot get enough money, enough help, a decent reception. If we finally get a good crowd, it snows or there is a hurricane, and nobody can come. This God of ours is not predictable.

This is what the parables point out. They try to prepare our minds for a different set of expectations from the ones we bring with us from early childhood, and which social custom and even our religious group support.

Paul was thinking, "I'm working for you, Lord, risking my life for you, and this sting of the flesh is getting me down. Can't you do something about it?" There has been much scholarly discussion about what this "sting of the flesh" might have been. It was not an abstract problem; it was in his flesh. Maybe he had arthritis. Maybe he had an emotional problem. Maybe his was an aggressive personality that kept alienating his beloved disciples. Maybe he was impetuous and had a sharp tongue. Whatever it was, it was serious. He besought the Lord again and again saying, "Let me out of this mess. Help! Help!" And the reply came, "Nothing doing. I prefer the way things are. My power is made perfect in weakness."

This is news. God is more pleased with our weakness than our success. Why? Perhaps because for most people success is self-defeating. Until we have been squashed, stepped on, rejected, opposed, persecuted, and have endured all kinds of difficulties, success is hard to handle. The experience of our weakness is God's special gift.

—*The Kingdom of God Is Like . . .*

Prayer

O Holy Spirit, may Your Gift of Fortitude
uphold us in times of trial and temptation, and
enable us to never give up, give in, or run away.

FORGIVENESS

Matthew 18:21-22

*Peter came and said to [Jesus], "Lord, if
another member of the church sins against me,
how often should I forgive? As many as seven
times?" Jesus said to him, "Not seven times,
but, I tell you, seventy-seven times."*

The teaching being presented has a certain vigor. Jesus
tells Peter, "Not only should you forgive your brother
seven times, but any number of times." This is a new way
of thinking about forgiveness. Human beings have felt
from time immemorial that if they are offended, they are
entitled to revenge. Revenge resists the open-heartedness to
which the gospel calls us.

In this parable, the importance of forgiveness as the
essential healing of a bond that has been injured emerges in
full force. The health and integrity of every community, its
creativity and growth, depends on the sense of belonging.
Forgiveness is a necessity from this perspective; it is the
very fabric of the universe.

The outstretched arms of Jesus on the cross are the
symbol of the forgiveness of everything and everyone. This
love triumphs over the forces of entropy in creation. In a

sense, unwillingness to forgive is an attack upon God. God is so identified with creation that any unwillingness to forgive is a resistance to grace; any movement to injure another is to tear God to pieces.

The bond of love needs to be constantly renewed. Forgiveness maintains and strengthens the bond of unity that enables all life to grow. If we have much to forgive, we also have much to be forgiven. The proportion between the two, the parable suggests, is very small.

—*Awakenings*

Prayer

Holy Spirit of God, may Your precious Fruits of charity, joy, and peace abound in us.

SPIRITUAL ATTENTIVENESS

Deuteronomy 4:9

*Take care and watch yourselves closely, so as
neither to forget the things that your eyes have
seen nor to let them slip from your mind all the
days of your life; make them known to your
children and your children's children.*

As we cultivate the friendship of Christ, a point comes
when we too may move beyond the particular words of the
gospel to the person who is speaking, the eternal Word
incarnate in Jesus and disclosing himself to us in the text.
. . . When we are alert to the person of Christ speaking to
us through the text, we have reached a point of spiritual
attentiveness. The purpose of every true devotional practice
and method of prayer is to bring us to a person-to-person,
being-to-being relationship with Christ. This involves
relating not just to the words of Jesus or to the details of his
physical presence, but to the *person* of Jesus, the eternal
Word in human form.

Little by little, spiritual attentiveness—this not-
knowing by means of concepts and emotions—becomes
habitual. The presence of God insinuates itself into our
awareness in prayer and continues to unfold. It is at this
point that the Fathers of the Church offer their teaching

about the spiritual senses to help us understand the riches hidden in spiritual attentiveness. They spoke of the initial experience of the perception of God's presence as perfume. This they attributed to the spiritual sense of smell. Smell, as one of the external senses, is the attraction or aversion that one experiences when a delightful or disagreeable odor is in the neighborhood. It does not take long for the olfactory apparatus to say yes or no to a particular scent. If it is wisteria or perfume, it is charming; if it is garlic or something unpleasant, you move to another room.

—Crisis of Faith, Crisis of Love

Prayer

Holy Spirit of God, You fill the earth and all creation with Your Presence. Make us feel our oneness with all that You have made.

INTERIOR SILENCE

Psalm 95:7-9

O that today you would listen to his voice!
Do not harden your hearts, as at Meribah,
as on the day at Massah in the wilderness,
when your ancestors tested me,
and put me to the proof, though they had
seen my work.

In human relationships, as mutual love deepens, there comes a time when the two friends convey their sentiments without words. They can sit in silence sharing an experience or simply enjoying each other's presence without saying anything. Holding hands or a single word from time to time can maintain this deep communication.

This loving relationship points to the kind of interior silence that is being developed in contemplative prayer. The goal of contemplative prayer is not so much the emptiness of thoughts or conversation as the emptiness of self. In contemplative prayer we cease to multiply reflections and acts of the will. A different kind of knowledge rooted in love emerges in which the awareness of God's presence supplants the awareness of our own presence and the inveterate tendency to reflect on ourselves. The experience of God's presence frees us from making ourself or our relationship with God the center of the universe. The language of the mystics must not be taken literally when they speak of emptiness or the void. Jesus practiced emptiness in becoming a human being, emptying himself of his prerogatives and the natural consequences of his divine dignity. The void does not mean void in the sense of a vacuum, but void in the sense of attachment to our own activity. Our own reflections and acts of will are necessary preliminaries to getting acquainted with Christ, but have to be transcended if Christ is to share his most personal prayer to the Father, which is characterized by total self-surrender.

—Intimacy with God

Prayer

O Holy Spirit, we have no capacity to perceive
You as You really are. Be Yourself, the
continuous revealing of the Mystery of Your
Presence.

THE GREAT COMMANDMENT

Mark 12:28-31

*One of the scribes came near and heard them
disputing with one another, and seeing that
[Jesus] answered them well, he asked him,
"Which commandment is the first of all?"
Jesus answered, "The first is, 'Hear, O Israel:
the Lord our God, the Lord is one; you shall
love the Lord your God with all your heart, and
with all your soul, and with all your mind, and
with all your strength.' The second is this, 'You
shall love your neighbor as yourself.' There is
no other commandment greater than these."*

What Jesus is saying to this young scribe is that his
abstract understanding of the primary precept of the Old
Testament is "right on" and that if he pursues that course,
the values of the false-self system are gradually freed from
their fascination with pleasure, power, and security. One
then moves into the awareness of the presence of God
within. With that movement comes the capacity to love
God with our whole mind, heart, soul, and strength.

By accessing the mystery of God's presence within, we
are capable of perceiving the presence of God in others.
The presence of God in us recognizes the presence of God

in everyone else. Then it is possible to love them as
ourselves.

The second precept flows automatically from the first.
If we truly love God, we can love our neighbor as we love
the true self that we have found through the process of
liberation. The whole movement from the tyranny of Egypt
to the promised land in the book of Exodus is a parable of
the movement from the tyranny of the false self through the
desert of purification into the promised land of interior
freedom.

There is an intriguing second section to this text.
Although Jesus approved of the first commandment and its
corollary to love one's neighbor as oneself and congratu-
lated the young man on his insight, he also said, "You are
not far from the kingdom of God." In other words, the
kingdom of God requires something more than to love our
neighbor as ourselves. To love our neighbor from the
perspective of the true self, as one possessing the image of
God, is a great insight, but it still is not the fullness of the
kingdom of God according to Jesus.

A new commandment characterizes the Christian faith
that carries the insight of the scribe a step further. It is to
love one another *as Jesus has loved us.* This is much more
difficult. This is to love others in their individuality,
uniqueness, personality traits, temperamental biases,
personal history, and in the things that drive us up the wall,
to love our neighbor, in other words, just as they are with
each one's grocery list of faults, unbearable habits, unrea-
sonable demands, and impossible characteristics. The new

commandment is to accept others unconditionally; that is to say, without the least wish to change them. To love them in their individuality is the way Jesus has loved us. He gives us the space in which to change and the time to confront the obstacles that prevent further change.

—Awakenings

Prayer

O Holy Spirit, whom the Father has sent to instruct us in all things, teach us to live our ordinary lives with extraordinary love.

THE SACRED IN THE SECULAR

Luke 18:10-14

*Two men went up to the temple to pray, one a
Pharisee and the other a tax collector. The
Pharisee, standing by himself, was praying
thus, "God, I thank you that I am not like other
people: thieves, rogues, adulterers, or even like
this tax collector. I fast twice a week; I give a
tenth of all my income." But the tax collector,
standing far off, would not even look up to
heaven, but was beating his breast and saying,
"God, be merciful to me, a sinner!" I tell you,
this man went down to his home justified rather
than the other.*

The parable of the publican and the Pharisee reinforces
one of the central themes of the parable of the good Samaritan. The coming of the good Samaritan down the road to
Jericho signals the end of the social landscape and map of
the kingdom of God as perceived by Jesus' contemporaries.

The two men described in the parable manifest their
relative places and status in the accepted culture of the time.
One belongs to the sacred precincts of the temple and is an
insider. The other belongs to the secular world and is an

outsider. The social map calls for him to pray apart from the Pharisee, who represents the holy. Thus from the text there is no evidence of merit or blame in the conduct or prayers of the two men.

The storyteller stuns the hearers with his conclusion: "The publican went home to his house (to the secular world) justified. The other man did not." These words come like a peal of thunder to the crowd. Luke attributes this statement to the humility of the publican and to the pride of the Pharisee, but the publican did not even make restitution for his extortions . . . and the Pharisee thanked God for his good deeds, as was customary in the prayers of a devout Pharisee of his time.

Thus the main point of the parable emerges with stark clarity. The social map of the time is being abandoned and the kingdom of God is no longer to be found in the temple. The holy is outside and the unholy may be inside. The activity of the kingdom of God has moved from the sacred precincts of the temple to the profane area of the secular world. The Pharisee represents well the piety of the temple. The publican represents well the secular world. The sacred place is no longer the place of the sacred. The sacred has moved to everyday life.

—*The Kingdom of God is Like . . .*

Prayer

Holy Spirit of God, may Your divine Love, so firm and yet so tender, purify our inmost being to its very roots and bring us to true humility of heart.

SPIRITUAL BLINDNESS

John 9:1, 6-7

*As [Jesus] walked along, he saw a man blind
from birth. [Jesus] spat on the ground and
made mud with the saliva and spread the mud
on the man's eyes, saying to him, "Go, wash in
the pool of Siloam" (which means Sent). Then
he went and washed and came back able to see.*

To look at this blind man begging for food is for Jesus
an acute pain. Naturally he wants to do something about it.
Notice what he does. He spits on the ground. We read in
the scriptures that Yahweh breathed the breath of life into
the first man. Jesus also breathed on his disciples after his
resurrection, bestowing upon them the fullness of the
Spirit.

Breathing is a symbol of the bestowal of the Spirit
(The word "spirit" means breath). Saliva also represents
the bestowal of the Spirit. Jesus mixes his spittle with dirt,
making a mud pie. He then anoints the eyes of the blind
man with the mud, symbolizing the Incarnation of the
Word made flesh.

The text points to the healing of the human predicament, which is seeking happiness in the wrong places.
Happiness is re-bonding with the divine presence and

action within. A new dimension has been introduced into the human family. Not only is divine intimacy restored but infinitely more is given.

Easter is the superabundant joy in the new gift of God that transcends the original plan. God himself becomes part of the human family in order that we may participate in the divine life, not as something given from outside, but as something that inherently belongs to us as human beings through solidarity with Jesus Christ. This idea of solidarity with God through Jesus Christ, the divine human being, describes the mystical intuition of the unity of the human family.

—Reawakenings

Prayer

O Holy Spirit, help us to embrace every human being as the child of God, and to manifest Your Love for one another.

CRISIS OF FAITH

John 4:46-53

*[Jesus] came again to Cana in Galilee where
he had changed the water into wine. Now there
was a royal official whose son lay ill in
Capernaum. When he heard that Jesus had
come from Judea to Galilee, he went and
begged him to come down and heal his son, for
he was at the point of death. Then Jesus said to
him, "Unless you see signs and wonders you
will not believe." The official said to him, "Sir,
come down before my little boy dies." Jesus
said to him, "Go; your son will live." The man
believed the word that Jesus spoke to him and
started on his way. As he was going down, his
slaves met him and told him that his child was
alive. So he asked them the hour when be
began to recover, and they said to him,
"Yesterday at one in the afternoon the fever left
him." The father realized that this was the hour
when Jesus had said to him, "Your son will
live." So he himself believed, along with his
whole household.*

There are two great crises in the process of spiritual
maturity. The centers of gravitation around which these two

crises revolve are faith and love. . . . The emphasis in the
first crisis is on the growth, purification, and strengthening
of our faith. . . .

In John's gospel we have the following scene. Jesus
was on his way to Cana. Along came a royal official from
Capernaum, pleading, "Come down and heal my son!"
Jesus showed great reluctance to go, saying, "Unless you
see striking signs of power, you do not believe." But the
man cried out in desperation, "Sir, come down now. My
son is on the point of death!" Jesus replied, "You go. Your
son is healed." The man went down and at the same hour—
the Gospel is careful to bring that point out—the very
moment Jesus uttered the words, the fever left the boy.

[This man] believed in the power of Jesus' presence.
His weak faith required the physical presence of Jesus. He
did not apparently believe that Jesus could heal his little
son without coming down and physically laying his hands
upon him. He is a symbol of those who need to feel the
sensible presence of the Lord, at least from time to time, to
sustain their faith. And what does Jesus do? He refuses to
go down.
Why? Because the absence of his physical presence is
to be the occasion of increasing this man's faith. When the
royal official went back to Capernaum believing in Jesus'
word and found that everything was as Jesus had said, then
he came to believe in the power of his word alone. I repeat,
the absence of the felt presence of the Lord is his normal

means of increasing our faith and of getting us to the point
of believing in the power of his word alone, without "signs
and wonders," that is to say, without the feeling of his
presence or external props.

It is a crisis of faith that he puts the royal official
through, and with great success. From that time on, he
believed. In fact, his whole household got the benefit of his
growth in faith.

—Crisis of Faith, Crisis of Love

Prayer

*Holy Spirit of God, may the Love which You
pour forth in our hearts cast out all fear.*

OUR CROSS

John 5:2-9

*In Jerusalem by the Sheep Gate there is a pool,
called in Hebrew Beth-zatha, which has five
porticoes. In these lay many invalids—blind,
lame, and paralyzed. One man was there who
had been ill for thirty-eight years. When Jesus
saw him lying there and knew that he had been
there a long time, he said to him, "Do you want
to be made well?" The sick man answered him,
"Sir, I have no one to put me into the pool
when the water is stirred up; and while I am
making my way, someone else steps down
ahead of me." Jesus said to him, "Stand up,
take your mat and walk." At once the man was
made well, and he took up his mat and began
to walk.*

There is no way of getting well from the wounds of our
early childhood except through the cross. The cross that
God asks us to accept is primarily our own pain that we
bring with us from early childhood. Our own wounds, our
own limitations, our own personality defects, all the
damage that people have done to us from the beginning of
life until now, and our personal experience of the pain of

the human condition as we individually have experienced it—that is our true cross! That is what Christ asks us to accept and to allow him to share. Actually in his passion he has already experienced our pain and made it his own. In other words, we simply enter into something that has already happened, namely, our union with Christ and all that it implies, his taking into himself all of our pain, anxiety, fears, self-hatred, and discouragement.

It is all included implicitly in his cry on the cross, "My God, why have you abandoned me?" That is the big question. Here is God's son, the beloved, to whom we are to listen—Christ who has based his whole mission and ministry on his relationship with the Father—and it has all disappeared. His disciples have fled. His message is torn to shreds. He stands condemned by the religious and Roman authorities. There is nothing left of his message, humanly speaking. Yet this is the moment of our redemption. Why? Because his cry on the cross is our cry of a desperate alienation from God, taken up into his, and transformed into resurrection. As we sit there and sweat it out and allow the pain to come up, we realize that it is Christ suffering in us and redeeming us.

—*Intimacy with God*

Prayer

O Holy Spirit, infinite outpouring of the Love
of the Father and the Son, soothe the wounds
the refining fire of Your Love has cauterized.

DEEP REST

Isaiah 49:13

Sing for joy, O heavens, and exult, O earth;
break forth, O mountains, into singing!
For the Lord has comforted his people,
and will have compassion on his suffering
ones.

"Rest" is the term for a wide variety of psychological impressions, such as peace, interior silence, contentment, a sense of coming home, of well-being, and most of all, of God's presence. Suppose this rest is so deep that at some point during prayer there are few or no thoughts passing by. Or one has a strong sense of the presence of God. The experience of deep rest . . . automatically causes the body to rest, and indeed to rest in a greater degree than in sleep.

The feeling of deep rest, especially when it involves a deep sense of the divine presence, leads to a kind of psychological transference with God. That is to say, God becomes the therapist in the psychoanalytic sense in which we look to a therapist for the trust and love that we did not feel we received as a child from an important other, such as a parent.

Deep rest is not only the result of freedom from attachments or aversions to thoughts, but also the feeling of

being accepted and loved by the divine Mystery that we
sense within us and that Christian doctrine calls the Divine
Indwelling. In other words, our awareness of the divine
presence begins to reawaken.

Rest grows deeper as our trust in God deepens, and the
emotional doubts about our self-worth, impressed upon us
in early childhood by various rejections or excessive
competition with other siblings, begin to relax. Because the
rest is so profound, the body rests as never before.

—*Intimacy with God*

Prayer

*O Holy Spirit, in the struggle to surrender
ourselves completely to You, be our repose in
the depths of our hearts in the face of every
difficulty.*

SEPARATION FROM GOD

Psalm 106:19-21

They made a calf at Horeb
and worshiped a cast image.
They exchanged the glory of God
for the image of an ox that eats grass.
They forgot God, their Savior,
who had done great things in Egypt.

We are made for happiness and there is nothing wrong in reaching out for it. Unfortunately, most of us are so deprived of happiness that as soon as it comes along, we reach out for it with all our strength and try to hang on to it for dear life. That is the mistake. The best way to receive it is to give it away. If you give everything back to God, you will always be empty, and when you are empty, there is more room for God.

The experience of God usually comes as something you feel you have experienced before. God is so well suited to us that any experience of Him is a feeling of completion or well-being. What was lacking in us seems to be somehow mysteriously restored. This experience awakens confidence, peace, joy, and reverence all at the same time. Of course, the next thing that occurs to us is: "This is great! How am I going to hang on to it?" That's the normal human reaction. But experience teaches that that is exactly the worst thing to do. The innate tendency to hang on, to possess, is the biggest obstacle to union with God. The reason we are possessive is that we feel separated from God. The feeling of separation is our ordinary psychological experience of the human condition. This misapprehension is the cause of our efforts to look for happiness down every path that we can possibly envision, when actually it is right under our noses. We just don't know how to perceive it. Since the security that we should have as beings united with God is missing, we reach out to bolster up our fragile self-image with whatever possessions or power symbols we can lay hold of. In returning to God, we take the reverse path, which is to let go of all that we want to possess. Since nothing is more desirable than the feeling of God's presence, that, too, has to be a thought we are willing to let go of.

—*Open Mind, Open Heart*

Prayer

Come, Holy Spirit, Gift of the Father and the Son, fill us with the fullness of the life of the Trinity.

SUFFERING AND SACRIFICE

Psalm 34:17-18

*When the righteous cry for help, the Lord
    hears,
    and rescues them from all their troubles.
The Lord is near to the brokenhearted,
    and saves the crushed in spirit.*

    Sacrifice is absolutely essential for human growth; yet the abiding disposition of sacrifice is rarely established without some experience of suffering. Of course suffering itself does not make one holy and can even lead to despair. Despair is suffering that fails to teach.

    A clear distinction must be made between sacrifice and suffering. Suffering is the conscious experience of pain. Sacrifice can also involve conscious pain, but it is primarily an attitude. The attitude of sacrifice can transform suffering into joy. We bring many needless sufferings on ourselves, and these God does not will. But to suffer as a member of a fallen race and to endure the consequences of the human condition is what the Son of God himself did. This form of suffering may be an important part of our purification. God may also send suffering to people who are already thoroughly purified as a counterweight to the effects of moral evil in the world. This is called vicarious suffering. Most of the great religions of the world recognize this mystery.

The mystery of vicarious suffering is most clearly revealed in the crucifixion of Jesus Christ. There innocence itself was destroyed in order to redeem the human family. If God's only-begotten Son can suffer and die, the suffering and death of the innocent take on a wholly new dimension. It likewise can be seen as redemptive. Faith alone can perceive God triumphing in the midst of human suffering and bringing about the reign of divine love.

Suffering and death are not enemies, but doors leading to new levels of knowledge and love. Unless we are willing to sacrifice what we have now, we cannot grow. We grow by dying and rising again, by dying to where we are now and being reborn at a new level.

—*The Heart of the World*

Prayer

*O Holy Spirit, grant us that invincible trust in
You that only You can give.*

DIVINE GUIDANCE

Jeremiah 11:18

*It was the Lord who made it known to me,
and I knew.*

The old-fashioned guidance systems to keep airplanes on course during flight might help us to understand the art of listening to the divine guidance of the Holy Spirit. When the pilot is on course, he will not hear anything on his headphones. If he veers a little to the right, he will get a beep. If he goes too far the other way, he will pick up a different signal. By correcting his course, his headphones return to silence.

In the moment-by-moment process of daily life, similar indications of being on- or off-course are available. Any sign that you are upset is an invitation to ask yourself why you are upset and not to project the blame onto another person or the situation. Even if they are to blame, it won't do you any good until you solve the real problem, which resides in you. The fundamental work of a spiritual director of contemplatives is to encourage and to guide them to submit to the divine therapy, which allows the unconscious emotional material of early life that led to the drive for security, esteem and affection, and power symbols in the culture to be evacuated.

81

Each of us has a significant dose of the human condition. In Catholic theology we call it the consequences of original sin. We come into the world not knowing what true happiness is but needing it; not knowing what true affection is but needing it; not knowing what true freedom is but needing it. We bring with us into adult life the way we as children coped with impossible situations, either through repression of feelings or by compensatory programs for happiness that cannot possibly work. The stronger those needs, the more frustration when they are not fulfilled.

Into this universal human situation Jesus comes, saying, "Repent," which means "change the direction in which you are looking for happiness." Human happiness is found in the growth of unconditional love. The work of spiritual direction is to help us to become aware of the obstacles to divine love and the free circulation of that love within us. This requires the cultivation of a non-possessive attitude toward ourselves and other people. Gradually we learn that God is the true security, God truly loves us, and with this love, we can make it, even if no one else seems to care.

—*Contemplative Outreach News,* Summer, 1997

Prayer

Holy Spirit of God, by Your special Grace help us to surrender our false selves completely to You, and to relinquish every possessive attitude toward our actions.

CHRISTIAN AWAKENING

John 11:17, 20-23

*When Jesus arrived, he found that Lazarus had
already been in the tomb four days. When
Martha heard that Jesus was coming, she went
and met him, while Mary stayed at home.
Martha said to Jesus, "Lord, if you had been
here, my brother would not have died. But even
now I know that God will give you whatever
you ask of him." Jesus said to her, "Your
brother will rise again."*

The story of Lazarus is a preview of Jesus' approaching death and resurrection. Lazarus stands for fallen human race about to be raised from the death of sin to life in God through Christ's passion, death, and resurrection. The illness which Jesus allows Lazarus to undergo is the symbol of our false self with all its weakness, ignorance, and pride, together with all the damage lying in the unconscious from earliest childhood to the present moment. To raise Lazarus from this illness to life in the Spirit is the most profound meaning of the event. Lazarus's resurrection manifests the full significance of Christ's resurrection, which restores sinful humanity, not only to the divine life, but to its superabounding fullness.

Jesus hints at the special character of Lazarus's illness in these words: "This illness will not result in death, but will promote the glory of God." Lazarus represents in a special way those who seek to penetrate the mystery of Christ to its depth. The disposition is manifested by a willingness to die to the false self and to wait in patience for the inner resurrection, which can only come from Christ.

—*Crisis of Faith, Crisis of Love*

Prayer

O deliriously happy Light, fill to the uttermost
recesses the hearts of Your faithful children.

THE ADULTEROUS WOMAN

John 8:3-7

The scribes and the Pharisees brought a woman who had been caught in adultery; and making her stand before all of them, they said to him, "Teacher, this woman was caught in the very act of committing adultery. Now in the law Moses commanded us to stone such women. Now what do you say?" They said this to test him, so that they might have some charge to bring against him. Jesus bent down and wrote with his finger on the ground. When they kept on questioning him, he straightened up and said to them, "Let anyone among you who is without sin be the first to throw a stone at her."

Jesus' enemies were not interested in this unfortunate woman; she just happened to serve their purposes. Her sin provided them with what seemed like the perfect trap in which to catch Jesus. Whichever way he answered their carefully prepared question, they were sure he would be in trouble. If he said, "Yes, stone her," he would be going against the compassionate teaching he had been giving. If he said, "Don't stone her," they could say that he was not upholding the Law of Moses. He could then be brought before the authorities and accused of denigrating the Law. They thought they had Jesus wrapped up.

So they dragged the woman in front of him as he was teaching in the Temple precincts and said, "This woman has been caught in the act of adultery. The Law of Moses has ordered such women to be stoned. What is your opinion?" Their hypocrisy was clear. Not only were they representing themselves as righteous observers of the Law, but they were using the observance of the Law as an excuse to bring about Jesus' destruction.

The people hanging on Jesus' words were shocked and waited with bated breath to hear what he would answer. But he said nothing. Instead he bent down and started writing with his finger in the sand. What did this gesture mean? We read that God wrote the Ten Commandments with his finger on stone tablets. Perhaps Jesus was subtly affirming his divine authority as he wrote with his finger in the sand.

When they persisted, Jesus straightened up and said, "Let the person who has no sin be the first to cast a stone at her." Thus, he did not deny them the right to carry out this prescription of the Law, but he insisted on one condition, namely, that they have no sin on their consciences. Then he bent down and continued doodling.

The crowd began to thin out. The elders were the first to recognize that they could not throw any stones under the condition that Jesus had imposed. The younger zealots of the Law were the last to go. At last, Jesus and the woman were left alone.

Jesus looked up and said, "Woman, where are they?" Notice the irony of the question: "Has no one condemned you?" Evidently, the self-righteous observers of the Law, so eager to throw stones, could not measure up to the requirement that Jesus had laid down.

The woman answered, "No one." Jesus said, "Neither do I condemn you."

—Reawakenings

Prayer

O Holy Spirit, may the holy anointing of Your Presence teach us all truth and bring us to everlasting Life.

CONTEMPLATION

Psalm 102:1-2

Hear my prayer, O Lord;
  let my cry come to you.
Do not hide your face from me
  in the day of my distress.
Incline your ear to me;
  answer me speedily in the day when I call.

Contemplative prayer is the world in which God can do anything. To move into that realm is the greatest adventure. It is to be open to the Infinite and hence to infinite possibilities. Our private, self-made worlds come to an end; a new world appears within and around us and the impossible becomes an everyday experience. Yet the world that prayer reveals is barely noticeable in the ordinary course of events.

Christian life and growth are founded on faith in our own basic goodness, in the being that God has given us with its transcendent potential. This gift of being is our true Self. Through our consent by faith, Christ is born in us and He and our true Self become one. Our awakening to the presence and action of the Spirit is the unfolding of Christ's resurrection in us.

All true prayer is based on the conviction of the presence of the Spirit in us and of his unfailing and continual inspiration. Every prayer in this sense is prayer in the Spirit. Still, it seems more accurate to reserve the term "prayer in the Spirit" for that prayer in which the inspiration of the Spirit is given directly to our spirit without the intermediary of our own reflections or acts of will. In other words, the Spirit prays in us and we consent. The traditional term for this kind of prayer is "contemplation."

—*Open Mind, Open Heart*

Prayer

Come, Holy Spirit, pour into our hearts from the depths of the Trinity a ray of Your Light.

TRANSFORMING UNION

John 8:31-32

If you continue in my word, you are truly my disciples; and you will know the truth, and the truth will make you free.

There is a difference between "being" and "doing." Once one's being is transformed into Christ, all one's doing becomes anointed with the interior transformation of one's being. . . . This is the kind of transformation contemplative prayer tends to produce. It is easy to bog down at lower levels of spiritual development. The challenge always comes to go farther, and if we accept, we are off to the races again.

No one ever grew as much in the spiritual life as the Blessed Virgin Mary because there was no interior obstacle to hinder her growth. Growing in grace for her meant growing in the midst of the human condition with its interminable trials. She had, in fact, the heaviest kinds of trials. The transforming union should enable one to handle greater trials than those of less evolved Christians. What's the use of building this magnificent spiritual building unless you do something with it? I am sure God doesn't intend merely to look at these people who are so holy. He wants them to do something. If He liberated them from their false selves, it was precisely for some great purpose.

Life, once one is in union with God, is what God wants it to be. It is full of surprises. You can be sure that whatever you expect to happen will not happen. That is the only thing of which you can be certain in the spiritual journey. It is by giving up all your expectations that you will be led to Medicine Lake, the Native American's term for contemplative prayer. The medicine that everyone needs is contemplation, which alone leads to transformation.

—Open Mind, Open Heart

Prayer

O Holy Spirit, may those whom you have called and led into the transforming union be guided into unity of spirit with the Godhead.

DIVINE LOVE

Genesis 17:7

*I will establish my covenant between me and
you, and your offspring after you throughout
their generations, for an everlasting covenant,
to be God to you and to your offspring after
you.*

Divine love is not a feeling of benevolence. It is not a
feeling at all. It is *total* self-giving. There is no self-interest
in the Trinity. Each person of the Trinity dwells in the
others, and everything that they have is shared in common.
The only distinction is the way in which each shares the
infinite treasure of the Godhead. The Father shares it to
give it, the Son to receive it, and the Holy Spirit to rejoice
in it as the gift of the Father and the Son. When divine love
invades the world of broken people, a world in which there
is suffering and limitation, it is certain to be rejected. It is
precisely by being rejected, and yet still remaining steadfast in boundless compassion, that its divine character is
ultimately proved. Moreover, divine love triumphs over
every obstacle, including suffering and death. This is why
the passion of Jesus is the most magnificent and compre-
hensive revelation of divine love that exists. It reveals the

ultimate meaning of reality, which is sacrifice. In a world of imperfection, divine love is proved by sacrifice.

—The Heart of the World

Prayer

Holy Spirit of God, through the intercession of St. Thérèse of Lisieux, Doctor of the Church, grant us Your own divine Love with which to love You.

INTERIOR FREEDOM

Jeremiah 20:11,13

The Lord is with me like a dread warrior;
therefore my persecutors will stumble
and they will not prevail.
They will be greatly shamed,
for they will not succeed.
Their eternal dishonor
will never be forgotten.
Sing to the Lord;
praise the Lord!
For he has delivered the life of the needy
from the hands of evildoers.

There is no commandment that says we have to be upset by the way other people treat us. The reason we are upset is because we have an emotional program that says, "If someone is nasty to me, I cannot be happy or feel good about myself." It is true that there is psychological and sometimes physical pain involved in not being treated as a human being. In such situations, we have every right to be indignant and to take steps to remedy them. But apart from such circumstances, instead of reacting compulsively and retaliating, we could enjoy our freedom as human beings and refuse to be upset.

Once on the spiritual journey, we begin to perceive that our emotional programs for happiness prevent us from reacting to other people and their needs. When locked into our private worlds of narcissistic desires, we are not present to the needs of others when they seek help. The clarity with which we see other people's needs and respond to them is in direct proportion to our interior freedom.

—*Invitation to Love*

Prayer

O Holy Spirit, in all our temptations, calm our rebellious passions and quiet our fears when we feel overwhelmed.

FAITH

John 11:45

Many of the Jews therefore, who had come with Mary and had seen what Jesus did, believed in him.

Faith is the essential means of attaining salvation. We cannot reach faith by reasoning. It is like an intuition. We can prepare for it by reflection, by longing for it, and by pleading for it. But it can only come as a gift. Once it has been given, life assumes a new direction. A Christian is like someone getting on an elevator. Such a person is not interested in going anywhere horizontally; his or her desire is to go up.

If we conceptualize the Christian life as an ascent toward God, getting on an elevator for the first time and closing the door is an act of faith. We do not know what will happen. The door may open on the second, third, or fourth floor and, to our amazement, we find a new perspective of the world stretching out before us. After having enjoyed the vista on one floor, we get back on the elevator and enter once again into darkness. We have to make a new act of faith in order to get to the next level; that is, we have to go through the pain of passing through the transition from one level to the next.

Faith is not just the assent of our minds to a series of dogmas. Such a superficial view drains it of its full meaning. Faith is basically the surrender of our will. It is not a matter of understanding with our heads; it is the gift of our entire being to God—to the ultimate reality. It orients us definitively in God's direction.

—The Heart of the World

Prayer

O Holy Spirit, grant us an abiding awareness of Your boundless Presence, so all-embracing and yet free.

THE NEW CREATION

John 12:12-13

*The great crowd that had come to the festival
heard that Jesus was coming to Jerusalem. So
they took branches of palm trees and went out
to meet him, shouting,*
   "Hosanna!
   *Blessed is the one who comes in the name
      of the Lord—*
      the King of Israel!"

Jesus is the paradigm of humanity, the universal human
being, God's idea of human nature with its enormous
potentialities. According to the great hymn of Paul to God's
humility, the divine Person of the Word, source of everything that exists, did not cling to his divine dignity or
prerogatives, but threw them all away. In God there seems
to be the need not to be God. In creating, God, in a sense,
dies, because he is no longer alone; he is completely
involved in the evolution of these creatures whom he has
made so lovable.

   Christ emptied himself of the divine power that could
have protected him and opened himself in total vulnerability as he stretched out his arms on the cross to embrace all
human suffering. In the most real sense, we too are the
body of God; we too are a new humanity in which the

Word becomes flesh; we too can put ourselves in the service of the divine Word. Then God is experiencing human life through our senses, our emotions, and our thoughts. Each of us can give the eternal Word a new way in which he discovers his own infinite potentiality. Thus, God knows himself in us and experiences the human condition in all its ramifications. The Word lives in us, or more exactly, lives us. We are incorporated into the new creation that Christ has brought into the world by becoming a human being. We leave behind the false self and solidarity with Adam, which is solidarity in sin, death, and human misery. Jesus invites us to experience his consciousness of the Father, the Abba of infinite concern, the God who transcends both suffering and joy and manifests equally in both.

Christ on the donkey, waving aside the cheers of the crowd, is riding to his death. This is his way of revealing the heart of God once and for all in such a way that no one can ever doubt God's infinite mercy. The priest says over the bread and wine, "This is my Body." The power of those words extends to each of us as Christ awakens and celebrates his great sacrifice in our own hearts saying, "*You* are my body. *You* are my blood." You, with all of humanity, are a manifestation in the flesh of the new creation.

—Awakenings

Prayer

Come Holy Spirit, giver of divine Gifts, and share with us the supreme Gift, the Gift of Yourself.

THE ANOINTING AT BETHANY

John 12:1-3

*Six days before the Passover Jesus came to
Bethany, the home of Lazarus, whom he had
raised from the dead. There they gave a dinner
for him. Martha served, and Lazarus was one
of those at the table with him. Mary took a
pound of costly perfume made of pure nard,
anointed Jesus' feet, and wiped them with her
hair. The house was filled with the fragrance of
the perfume.*

The dinner at Bethany was given in honor of Jesus six
days before his passion and death. The Jewish authorities
were now plotting vigorously for his destruction. Judas had
already decided to betray him into the hands of his enemies. Simon the leper was the host at the dinner. Martha
was fulfilling her customary role as perfect hostess, and
Lazarus was one of the guests at table. It was an interesting
group of people: Jesus the Messiah, Mary the contemplative, Martha the activist, Simon the leper, Judas the thief,
and Lazarus the former corpse.

Everyone was reclining at table except Mary. When
she walked in, all eyes turned toward her. Everybody knew

she had a deep love for Jesus. She was carrying an alabaster jar in which there was a pound of nard perfume. A pound of nard perfume was extremely expensive. Later we learn that it was worth three hundred denarii, an amount that represented the ordinary workingman's wages for an entire year.

She entered the room carrying the alabaster jar filled to the brim with the precious nard perfume and came to where Jesus was reclining. Suddenly, without a word, she smashed the bottle and poured the entire contents over his head. Out poured a pound of the incredibly costly perfume. The delicious odor billowed forth, filling the whole house with its fragrance. John adds that Mary also anointed the feet of Jesus and wiped them with her hair.

Mary was aware of what was being plotted by the authorities and wanted to affirm the depth of her faith in Jesus in a way that could not possibly be misunderstood. Some gesture had to be made before it was too late. Everyone recognized that by anointing him with expensive perfume, the symbol of her love, she was expressing her devotion to him and manifesting the gift of herself. But the deepest meaning of her symbolic gesture was not simply the gift of herself, but the *totality* of that gift. Not only did she anoint him with the costly perfume; she smashed the bottle and emptied its entire contents over his head! She threw herself away, so to speak, emptying every last drop of the perfume in superabundant expression of the *total* gift of herself. This is the meaning of her extraordinary gesture as Jesus perceived it and which so moved him. "You always have the poor with you," he said, "but you do not always have me. She did what she could: by anointing my body, she prepared it for burial just in time."

In this remarkable incident, Mary manifests her intuition into what Jesus is about to do. Moreover, she identifies with him to such an intimate degree that she manifests the same disposition of total self-giving that he is about to manifest on the cross. She had learned from Jesus how to throw herself away and become like God. That is why this story must be proclaimed wherever the Gospel is preached. "To perpetuate Mary's memory" is to fill the whole world with the perfume of God's love, the love that is totally self-giving. In the concrete, it is to anoint the poor and the afflicted, the favored members of Christ's Body, with this love.

—*The Mystery of Christ*

Prayer

O Holy Spirit, through Your Gift of Counsel, be our companion in each moment of our lives so that we can manifest Your goodness in every action.

TRUST IN GOD

Psalm 71:1, 5-6

In you, O Lord, I take refuge;
let me never be put to shame.
For you, O Lord, are my hope,
my trust, O Lord, from my youth.
Upon you I have leaned from my birth;
it was you who took me from my mother's
womb.
My praise is continually of you.

In the book of Deuteronomy, Moses compares God's training of his people to an eagle training an eaglet to fly. In ancient times it was believed that eaglets learned to fly by being pushed out of the nest, which was usually perched on the edge of a cliff. This is a marvelous image of what we feel is happening to us. God seems to push us into something that we feel totally incapable of doing. We wonder if he still loves us. Or again, he pushes us out of whatever nest we are in. Like the eaglet desperately flapping its wings, we seem to be heading straight for the abyss. But like the mother eagle, God swoops down and catches us just before we hit the rocks. This happens again and again until the eaglet learns to fly.

After we have been treated in this fashion a number of times, we too may realize that it is not as dangerous as we first believed. We begin to be content with these hair-raising escapes. We learn to trust God beyond our psychological experiences. And we become more courageous in facing and letting go of the dark corners of ourselves and begin to participate actively in the dismantling of our prerational emotional programs.

—*Invitation to Love*

Prayer

*O Holy Spirit, may we know Your gentle touch
and the grip of Your protecting arm.*

SHEER VULNERABILITY

Isaiah 50:6-7

I gave my back to those who struck me,
and my cheeks to those who pulled out the
beard;
I did not hide my face
from insult and spitting.
The Lord God helps me;
therefore I have not been disgraced;
therefore I have set my face like flint,
and I know that I shall not be put to
shame.

The love of Christ manifested itself in his sheer vulnerability. The crucifix is the sign and expression of the total vulnerability of Jesus: the outstretched arms, the open heart, the forgiveness of everything and everyone. This sheer vulnerability made him wide open both to suffering *and* to joy.

It was this vulnerability that caused him to experience the pain of Judas's betrayal, as well as the joy of celebrating the Pasch with his disciples.

If there had been no possibility of betrayal, there could have been no Eucharist. If the disciples were to be admitted to his intimate friendship, there could only be loneliness and disappointment when they all abandoned him and fled. Only in the heart of one with boundless readiness to forgive could there have been the pain of Peter's triple denial, and afterwards the joy of reinstating him as chief of the apostles.

Vulnerability means to be hurt over and over again without seeking to love less, but more. Divine love is sheer vulnerability—sheer openness to giving. Hence, when it enters the world, either in the person of Jesus or in one of his disciples, it is certain to encounter persecution—death many times over. But it will also encounter the joy of ever rising again. "For love is stronger than death . . . Many waters cannot quench it" (Song of Songs 8:6-7). Being vulnerable means loving one another as Christ loved us. If we did not have to forgive people, we would have no way of manifesting God's forgiveness toward us. People who injure us are doing us a great favor because they are providing us with the opportunity of passing on the mercy that we have received. By showing mercy, we increase the mercy we receive. The best way to receive divine love is to give it away, and the more we pass on, the more we increase our capacity to receive.

—*The Heart of the World*

Prayer

Holy Spirit of God, Your Presence is greater
than all consolation whether human or divine.
Your Presence is always available to us. May
we by Your Grace, always be available to It.

THE LAST SUPPER

John 13:3-5

*Jesus, knowing that the Father had given all
things into his hands, and that he had come
from God and was going to God, got up from
the table, took off his outer robe, and tied a
towel around himself. Then he poured water
into a basin and began to wash the disciples'
feet and to wipe them with the towel that was
tied around him.*

The texts read in the liturgy during Lent provide us
with the means to understand the sacred mysteries of Holy
Week. We think of the penitent woman who washed our
Lord's feet with her tears and of Mary of Bethany who
anointed his feet with the perfumed oil. It was the custom
of the time to wash the feet of a guest, to offer him a kiss of
welcome, and to anoint his head with ointment. It was not
the custom, however, to kiss those feet or to wash them
with one's tears; nor to place precious ointment of great
price on the guest's feet rather than upon his head. Why
such extremes on the part of these two devoted women?

They evidently wished to show that he was no ordinary
guest. Surely the divine goodness, which praised the
extravagance of these two women, would not do less than

offer you and me the ordinary courtesies, if he invites us to his banquet table.

With this background in mind, we can understand why Jesus washed the feet of his disciples. They were to be his guests at the first eucharistic supper, just as we are his guests at the commemoration of it. This sharing in the body and blood of the God-Man is the pledge of a still greater banquet: the eating and drinking of immortal life and love at the eternal banquet of heaven, where our nourishment will be the divine essence itself.

But as guests at the banquet table of the Lord in this world, and as recipients of the divine hospitality, the disciples had to receive at least the ordinary marks of courtesy; that is, the washing of the feet, the kiss of welcome, and the anointing with oil.

These three acts form an organic whole. Omitting any one of them would have been to fail in courtesy, something the Father would never do to guests invited to his supper. These three marks of courtesy correspond to the three stages of Christian initiation.

First comes the washing of the feet, symbol of baptism, which must precede the Eucharist. The Eucharist represents the kiss of welcome, the intimacy of union, and the mutual sharing of deep love. The anointing of the head with perfumed oil suggests the grace of the sacrament of confirmation.

These reminders of the divine hospitality, of the inconceivable courtesy that God has extended to us, make us approach the Paschal Mystery with humble and grateful hearts. How can we thank the Lord for his invitation, for the incredible depth of his sharing?

—Awakenings

Prayer

Lord Jesus Christ, may we know the full extent of Your divine hospitality, which is the Gift of Your Holy Spirit.

THE PASCHAL MYSTERY

Isaiah 53:3-5, 10

He was despised and rejected by others;
a man of suffering and acquainted with
infirmity;
and as one from whom others hide their faces
he was despised, and we held him of no
account.
Surely he has borne our infirmities
and carried our diseases;
yet we accounted him stricken,
struck down by God, and afflicted.
But he was wounded for our transgressions,
crushed for our iniquities;
upon him was the punishment that made us
whole,
and by his bruises we are healed.
Yet it was the will of the Lord to crush him with
pain.
When you make his life an offering for sin,
he shall see his offspring, and shall
prolong his days;
through him the will of the Lord shall prosper.

To become sin is to cease to be God's son—or at least
to cease to be conscious of being God's son. To cease to be
conscious of being God's son is to cease to experience God
as Father. The cross of Jesus represents the ultimate death-
of-God experience: "My God, my God, why have You
forsaken me?" The crucifixion is much more than the
physical death of Jesus and the emotional and mental
anguish that accompanied it. It is the death of his relationship with the Father. The crucifixion was not the death of
his false self because he never had one. It was the death of
his deified self and the annihilation of the ineffable union
which he enjoyed with the Father in his human faculties.
This was more than spiritual death; it was dying to being
God and hence the dying *of* God: "He emptied himself, and
took the form of a slave . . . accepting even death, death on
a cross!" The loss of personal identity is the ultimate
kenosis.

In the crucifixion, his relationship with the Father
disappeared and with it the loss of his experience of *who*
the Father is. In his resurrection and ascension, Jesus
discovered *all that* the Father is, and in doing so, became
one with the Ultimate Reality: *all that God is* emerging
eternally from *all that God is.*

This passing of Jesus from human to divine subjectiv-
ity is called in Christian tradition the Paschal Mystery. Our
participation in this Mystery is the passing over of the
transformed self into the loss of self as a fixed point of
reference; of *who* God is into *all that* God is. The dismantling of the false self and the inward journey to the true self
is the first phase of this transition or passing over. The loss

of the true self as a fixed point of reference is the second
phase. The first phase results in the consciousness of
personal union with the Trinity. The second phase consists
in being emptied of this union and identifying with the
absolute nothingness from which all things emerge, to
which all things return, and which manifests Itself as *That-
Which-Is.*

—The Mystery of Christ [slightly revised]

Prayer

*Lord Jesus Christ, in Your death and descent
into hell You took away the sin of the world and
manifested the Father's infinite Love for us.
May we too enter into God's plan for the
redemption of the human family.*

THE BURIAL

Luke 23:50-56

*There was a good and righteous man named
Joseph, who, though a member of the council,
had not agreed to their plan and action. He
came from the Jewish town of Arimathea, and
he was waiting expectantly for the kingdom of
God. This man went to Pilate and asked for the
body of Jesus. Then he took it down, wrapped it
in a linen cloth, and laid it in a rock-hewn tomb
where no one had ever been laid. It was the day
of Preparation, and the sabbath was beginning.
The women who had come with him from
Galilee followed, and they saw the tomb and
how his body was laid. Then they returned, and
prepared spices and ointments.*

*On the sabbath they rested according to
the commandment.*

Jesus died on the day before the sabbath. His body was
taken down in a hurry and laid in the tomb. The sabbath
commemorates the seventh day of creation, the day God
rested from all his works. In honor of creation and at God's
express command, the Jewish people observed the sabbath
as a day of complete rest. But its most profound meaning is

contained in this particular sabbath in which, having laid down his life for the human family, Jesus, the Son of God, rested.

Out of respect for the death of the Redeemer, there is no liturgical celebration on Holy Saturday. In honor of Jesus' body resting in the tomb, the church also rests. There is nothing more to be said, nothing more to be done. On this day everything rests.

—*The Mystery of Christ*

Prayer

Father, Your Son Jesus Christ descended into hell, the ultimate experience of alienation from You in consequence of taking our sinfulness into Himself. You raised Him from the dead as the sign of Your forgiveness of everything and everyone. In the name of the Risen Christ, we ask for the grace of boundless confidence in Your Infinite Mercy.

ALLELUIA!

Responsorial Psalm of the Easter Vigil

Alleluia! Alleluia! Alleluia!

When you hear the triple "Alleluia" that introduces the Easter season in a burst of joy, what do you hear? What happens inside of you when you hear those thrilling acclamations?

Perhaps your thoughts revolve around the meaning of the word "Alleluia," recalling that it means something like "hurrah"—a cry of victory—and you reflect, "This is Easter! I must rejoice!" Perhaps some of you perceive a spontaneous joy at the thought of Christ's triumph over death; a peaceful sense of gratitude to God for his goodness; or a sense of how much he loves you, or how much you love him.

You may even experience something like a volcano exploding inside you—a tremendous burst of joyful energy coming from the deepest place inside of you, which causes you to forget all your own thoughts, the fatigue of the evening of the Paschal Vigil, and what happens afterward.

Anyone who responds to the sound of the "Alleluia" with the sheer experience of oneness with Christ has understood the resurrection. Those who have not yet experienced this union should have no doubt, no hesitation, that God is calling them to this experience. He is calling us, especially through this liturgical celebration of his resurrection, to become what baptism has already made us. Baptism has been done to us. We did nothing to bring it about—even if we were baptized as adults. It is the sheer gift of God. Eternal life has begun in us. We are the sons of God, incorporated into Christ's body. His Spirit dwells in us. All our sins are forgiven. The darkness of our ignorance and the weakness of our will are being healed. And if anything is lacking to us, Christ, who is interceding for us in heaven at the right hand of the Father, will give us that too.

We were responding to this intuition if, at the moment we heard the "Alleluia," we identified with Christ. He is ours by baptism. It only remains for us to become what we are and to enjoy what we possess.

—*Awakenings*

Prayer

Holy Spirit of God, as a mighty wind coming,
drench with grace our dried-out hearts. Pour
down torrents of mercy to wash away our sins
and to uproot every secret inclination that may
lead to sin. Renew and enhance in all who trust
in You Your sacred Seven Gifts.

ACKNOWLEDGMENTS

We wish to thank the following publishers for permission to reprint excerpts from previously published works by Thomas Keating:

From *Awakenings*, copyright © 1990 by St. Benedict's Abbey, Snowmass, Colorado. Reprinted by permission of The Crossroad Publishing Company. Material on pages 107-109 and 115-116 of this book previously appeared in the author's *And the World Was Made Flesh*, copyright © 1983 by Cistercian Abbey of Spencer, Inc.

From *Contemplative Outreach News*, copyright © 1988, 1996, and 1997 by St. Benedict's Monastery, Snowmass, Colorado. Reprinted by permission of Contemplative Outreach.

From *Crisis of Faith, Crisis of Love*, copyright © 1995 by St. Benedict's Monastery, Snowmass, Colorado. Reprinted by permission of The Continuum Publishing Company.

From *The Heart of the World*, copyright © 1999, 1983 by Cistercian Abbey of Spencer, Inc. Reprinted by permission of the author and The Crossroad Publishing Company.

From *Intimacy With God*, copyright © 1994 by St. Benedict's Monastery, Snowmass, Colorado. Reprinted by permission of The Crossroad Publishing Company.

OF RELATED INTEREST

Henri J.M. Nouwen
SHOW ME THE WAY
Readings for Each Day of Lent

"An excellent prayer starter for the Lenten Season"
—*Spiritual Book News*
0-8245-1353-3; $9.95

Therese Johnson Borchard, Editor
WOMAN, WHY ARE YOU WEEPING?
A Lenten Companion for Women

A prayer guide through each day of Lent,
organized by themes especially appropriate for women.
0-8245-1721-0; $9.95

*At your bookstore, or to order directly from the publisher,
please send check or money order (including $3.00 for the
first book plus $1.00 for each additional book) to:*

THE CROSSROAD PUBLISHING COMPANY
370 LEXINGTON AVENUE, NEW YORK, NY 10017

We hope you enjoyed JOURNEY TO THE CENTER.
Thank you for reading it.

crossroad